The Way of The Heart

The Way of The Heart

Henri J. M. Nouwen

DARTON · LONGMAN + TODD

First published in Great Britain in 1981 by
Darton, Longman and Todd Ltd
1 Spencer Court
140–142 Wandsworth High Street
London SW18 4JJ

Reprinted 1981, 1982, 1984 and 1987

2nd edition Daybreak, Darton, Longman and Todd 1990
2nd edition reprinted 1992

This edition Darton, Longman and Todd 1999

ISBN 0-232-52300-2

A catalogue record for this book is available
from the British Library.

Grateful acknowledgment is made to A. R. Mowbray &
Co. Ltd and Macmillan Publishing Co., Inc., for
permission to use excerpts from *The Sayings of the
Desert Fathers* translated by Benedicta Ward.

Designed by Sandie Boccacci
Phototypeset in 11½/15¼ pt Adobe Caslon
by Intype London Ltd
Printed and bound in Great Britain by
Page Bros, Norwich

To John Mogabgab

Contents

Acknowledgements

This book found its beginning in a seminar at Yale Divinity School on the spirituality of the desert. It was one of the most stimulating seminars I have ever been part of. We were five women and eleven men. We represented very different religious traditions: Unitarian, Disciples of Christ, Baptist, Presbyterian, Dutch Reformed, Christian Reformed, Episcopalian, Roman Catholic, and Greek Orthodox. In age we ranged from early twenties to late forties and in geographical background from the United States to Ireland, Holland, and Australia. Together we tried to discover what the Desert Fathers and Mothers of the fourth century have to say to men and women who want to be ministers of Jesus Christ in the twentieth century.

As we exchanged ideas and experiences in response to the stories from the desert, we gradually came to see the 'way of the heart' as the way that united us in spite of our many historical, theological, and psychological differences. It was this discovery that encouraged me to present 'the way of the heart' as

Convocation lectures at Perkins School of Theology in Dallas and at the National Convention of Pastoral Counselors in Denver. I am very grateful for the many responses I received during these occasions.

A special word of thanks goes to Virginia Yohe and Carol Plantinga for their secretarial assistance, to Stephen Leahy, Phil Zaeder, Fred Bratman, and Robert Moore for their editorial comments, and to John Eudes Bamberger for his encouragement.

I would also like to express my deep gratitude to all the members of the seminar: George Anastos, Kim Brown, Colman Cooke, Susan Geissler, Frank Gerry, Christine Koetsveld, Joseph Núñez, Robert Parenteau, Donald Postema, Kathy Stockton, Marjorie Thompson, Steven Tsichlis, Joshua Wootton, and Mich Zeman. Their many rich and varied responses to the words from the desert enabled me to present the book as a book for all who are committed to the Christian ministry.

I dedicate this book to John Mogabgab, who taught the course with me. I do so in gratitude not only for his invaluable contributions to the seminar and this book, but also, and most of all, for the five years during which we worked together at Yale Divinity School. His deep friendship and support have made these years a true gift of God.

Prologue

In ten years we will celebrate the second millennium of the Christian Era. But the question is: 'Will there be anything to celebrate?' Many voices wonder if humanity can survive its own destructive powers. As we reflect on the increasing poverty and hunger, the rapidly spreading hatred and violence within as well as between countries, and the frightening buildup of nuclear weapons systems, we come to realize that our world has embarked on a suicidal journey. We are painfully reminded of the words of John the Evangelist:

> The Word . . . the true light . . . was coming into the world . . . that had its being through him, and the world did not know him. He came to his own domain and his own people did not accept him (John 1:9–11).

It seems that the darkness is thicker than ever, that the powers of evil are more blatantly visible than ever, and that the children of God are being tested more severely than ever.

During the last few years I have been wondering

what it means to be a minister in such a situation. What is required of men and women who want to bring light into the darkness, 'to bring good news to the poor, to proclaim liberty to captives and to the blind new sight, to set the downtrodden free, to proclaim the Lord's year of favor' (Luke 4:18–19)? What is required of a man or a woman who is called to enter fully into the turmoil and agony of the times and speak a word of hope?

It is not difficult to see that in this fearful and painful period of our history we who minister in parishes, schools, universities, hospitals, and prisons are having a difficult time fulfilling our task of making the light of Christ shine into the darkness. Many of us have adapted ourselves too well to the general mood of lethargy. Others among us have become tired, exhausted, disappointed, bitter, resentful, or simply bored. Still others have remained active and involved – but have ended up living more in their own name than in the Name of Jesus Christ. This is not so strange. The pressures in the ministry are enormous, the demands are increasing, and the satisfactions diminishing. How can we expect to remain full of creative vitality, of zeal for the Word of God, of desire to serve, and of motivation to inspire our often numbed congregations? Where are we supposed to find nurture and strength? How can we alleviate our own spiritual hunger and thirst?

These are the concerns I should like to address in the following pages. I hope to offer some ideas and some disciplines that may be of help in our efforts to remain vital witnesses of Christ in the coming years; years that no doubt will be filled with temptations to unfaithfulness, a comfortable self-centeredness, and despair.

But where shall we turn? To Jacques Ellul, William Stringfellow, Thomas Merton, Teilhard de Chardin? They all have much to say, but I am interested in a more primitive source of inspiration, which by its directness, simplicity and concreteness, can lead us without any byways to the core of our struggle. This source is the *Apophthegmata Patrum*, the *Sayings of the Desert Fathers*. The Desert Fathers, who lived in the Egyptian desert during the fourth and fifth centuries, can offer us a very important perspective on our life as ministers living at the end of the twentieth century. The Desert Fathers – and there were Mothers, too – were Christians who searched for a new form of martyrdom. Once the persecutions had ceased, it was no longer possible to witness for Christ by following him as a blood witness. Yet the end of the persecutions did not mean that the world had accepted the ideals of Christ and altered its ways; the world continued to prefer the darkness to the light (John 3:19). But if the world was no longer the enemy of the Christian, then the Christian had to become the enemy of the dark world. The flight to the desert was the way to escape a tempting conformity to the world. Anthony, Agathon, Macarius, Poemen, Theodora, Sarah, and Syncletica became spiritual leaders in the desert. Here they became a new kind of martyr: witnesses against the destructive powers of evil, witnesses for the saving power of Jesus Christ.

Their spiritual commentaries, their counsel to visitors, and their very concrete ascetical practices form the basis of my reflections about the spiritual life of the minister in our day. Like the Desert Fathers and Mothers, we have to find a practical and workable response to Paul's exhortation: 'Do not model yourselves on the behavior of the world around you, but let your behavior change, modeled by your new mind. This is the only way to discover the will of God and know what is good, what it is that God wants, what is the perfect thing to do' (Romans 12:2).

To structure my reflections, I will use a story told about Abba Arsenius. Arsenius was a well-educated Roman of senatorial rank who lived at the court of Emperor Theodosius as tutor to the princes Arcadius and Honorius. 'While still living in the palace, Abba Arsenius prayed to God in these words, "Lord, lead me in the way of salvation." And a voice came saying to him, "Arsenius, flee from the world and you will be saved." Having sailed secretly from Rome to Alexandria and having withdrawn to the solitary life (in the desert) Arsenius prayed again: "Lord, lead me in the way of salvation" and again he heard a voice saying, "Arsenius, flee, be silent, pray always, for these are the sources of sinlessness." "[1] The words *flee, be silent* and *pray* summarize the spirituality of the desert. They indicate the three ways of preventing the world from shaping us in its image and are thus the three ways to life in the Spirit.

My first task is to explore what it means for us to flee from the world. This raises the question of solitude. My second task is to define silence as an essential element of a spirituality of ministry. Finally, I want to challenge you with the vocation to pray always.

Solitude

Introduction

St. Anthony, the 'father of monks,' is the best guide in our attempt to understand the role of solitude in ministry. Born around 251, Anthony was the son of Egyptian peasants. When he was about eighteen years old he heard in church the Gospel words, 'Go and sell what you own and give the money to the poor . . . then come and follow me' (Matthew 19:21). Anthony realized that these words were meant for him personally. After a period of living as a poor laborer at the edge of his village, he withdrew into the desert, where for twenty years he lived in complete solitude. During these years Anthony experienced a terrible trial. The shell of his superficial securities was cracked and the abyss of iniquity was opened to him. But he came out of this trial victoriously – not because of his own willpower or ascetic exploits, but because of his unconditional surrender to the Lordship of Jesus Christ. When he emerged from his solitude, people recognized in him the qualities of an authentic 'healthy' man, whole in body, mind, and soul. They flocked to him for healing, comfort, and direction. In his old age, Anthony retired to an even deeper solitude to be totally absorbed in direct communion with God. He died in the year 356, when he was about one hundred and six years old.

The story of St. Anthony, as told by St. Athanasius, shows that we must be made aware of the call to let our false, compulsive self be transformed into the new self of Jesus Christ. It also shows that solitude is the furnace in which this transformation takes place. Finally, it reveals that it is from this transformed or converted self that real ministry flows. I therefore propose to explore these three aspects of St. Anthony's life in the hope of uncovering the problems as well as the opportunities in our ministry.

The Compulsive Minister

Thomas Merton writes in the introduction to his *The Wisdom of the Desert:*

> Society . . . was regarded [by the Desert Fathers] as a shipwreck from which each single individual man had to swim for his life . . . These were men who believed that to let oneself drift along, passively accepting the tenets and values of what they knew as society, was purely and simply a disaster.[1]

This observation leads us straight to the core of the

problem. Our society is not a community radiant with the love of Christ, but a dangerous network of domination and manipulation in which we can easily get entangled and lose our soul. The basic question is whether we ministers of Jesus Christ have not already been so deeply molded by the seductive powers of our dark world that we have become blind to our own and other people's fatal state and have lost the power and motivation to swim for our lives.

Just look for a moment at our daily routine. In general we are very busy people. We have many meetings to attend, many visits to make, many services to lead. Our calendars are filled with appointments, our days and weeks filled with engagements, and our years filled with plans and projects. There is seldom a period in which we do not know what to do, and we move through life in such a distracted way that we do not even take the time and rest to wonder if any of the things we think, say, or do are *worth* thinking, saying, or doing. We simply go along with the many 'musts' and 'oughts' that have been handed on to us, and we live with them as if they were authentic translations of the Gospel of our Lord. People must be motivated to come to church, youth must be entertained, money must be raised, and above all everyone must be happy. Moreover, we ought to be on good terms with the church and civil authorities; we ought to be liked or at least respected by a fair majority of our parishioners;

we ought to move up in the ranks according to schedule; and we ought to have enough vacation and salary to live a comfortable life. Thus we are busy people just like all other busy people, rewarded with the rewards which are rewarded to busy people!

All this is simply to suggest how horrendously secular our ministerial lives tend to be. Why is this so? Why do we children of the light so easily become conspirators with the darkness? The answer is quite simple. Our identity, our sense of self, is at stake. Secularity is a way of being dependent on the responses of our milieu. The secular or false self is the self which is fabricated, as Thomas Merton says, by social compulsions. 'Compulsive' is indeed the best adjective for the false self. It points to the need for ongoing and increasing affirmation. Who am I? I am the one who is liked, praised, admired, disliked, hated or despised. Whether I am a pianist, a businessman or a minister, what matters is how I am perceived by my world. If being busy is a good thing, then I must be busy. If having money is a sign of real freedom, then I must claim my money. If knowing many people proves my importance, I will have to make the necessary contacts. The compulsion manifests itself in the lurking fear of failing and the steady urge to prevent this by gathering more of the same – more work, more money, more friends.

These very compulsions are at the basis of the two

main enemies of the spiritual life: anger and greed. They are the inner side of a secular life, the sour fruits of our worldly dependencies. What else is anger than the impulsive response to the experience of being deprived? When my sense of self depends on what others say of me, anger is a quite natural reaction to a critical word. And when my sense of self depends on what I can acquire, greed flares up when my desires are frustrated. Thus greed and anger are the brother and sister of a false self fabricated by the social compulsions of an unredeemed world.

Anger in particular seems close to a professional vice in the contemporary ministry. Pastors are angry at their leaders for not leading and at their followers for not following. They are angry at those who do not come to church for not coming and angry at those who do come for coming without enthusiasm. They are angry at their families, who make them feel guilty, and angry at themselves for not being who they want to be. This is not an open, blatant, roaring anger, but an anger hidden behind the smooth word, the smiling face, and the polite handshake. It is a frozen anger, an anger which settles into a biting resentment and slowly paralyzes a generous heart. If there is anything that makes the ministry look grim and dull, it is this dark, insidious anger in the servants of Christ.

It is not so strange that Anthony and his fellow monks considered it a spiritual disaster to accept passively the tenets and values of their society. They had come to appreciate how hard it is not only for the individual Christian but also for the church itself to escape the seductive compulsions of the world. What was their response? They escaped from the sinking ship and swam for their lives. And the place of salvation is called desert, the place of solitude. Let us now see what this solitude did to them.

The Furnace of Transformation

When Anthony heard the word of Jesus, 'Go and sell what you own and give the money to the poor . . . then come and follow me,' he took it as a call to escape from the compulsions of his world. He moved away from his family, lived in poverty in a hut on the edge of his village, and occupied himself with manual work and prayer. But soon he realized that more was required of him. He had to face his enemies – anger and greed – head-on and let himself be totally transformed into a new being. His old, false self had to die and a new self had to be born. For this Anthony withdrew into the complete solitude of the desert.

Solitude is the furnace of transformation. Without solitude we remain victims of our society and continue to be entangled in the illusions of the false self. Jesus himself entered into this furnace. There he was tempted with the three compulsions of the world: to be relevant ('turn stones into loaves'), to be spectacular ('throw yourself down'), and to be powerful ('I will give you all these kingdoms'). There he affirmed God as the only source of his identity ('You must worship the Lord your God and serve him alone'). Solitude is the place of the great struggle and the great encounter – the struggle against the compulsions of the false self, and the encounter with the loving God who offers himself as the substance of the new self.

This might sound rather forbidding. It might even evoke images of medieval ascetical pursuits from which Luther and Calvin have happily saved us. But once we have given these fantasies their due and let them wander off, we will see that we are dealing here with that holy place where ministry and spirituality embrace each other. It is the place called solitude.

In order to understand the meaning of solitude, we must first unmask the ways in which the idea of solitude has been distorted by our world. We say to each other that we need some solitude in our lives. What we really are thinking of, however, is a time and a place for ourselves in which we are not bothered by other people, can think our own thoughts, express our own complaints, and do our own thing, whatever it may be. For us, solitude most often means privacy. We have come to the dubious conviction that we all have a right to privacy. Solitude thus becomes like a spiritual property for which we can compete on the free market of spiritual goods. But there is more. We also think of solitude as a station where we can recharge our batteries, or as the corner of the boxing ring where our wounds are oiled, our muscles massaged, and our courage restored by fitting slogans. In short, we think of solitude as a place where we gather new strength to continue the ongoing competition in life.

But that is not the solitude of St. John the Baptist, of St. Anthony or St. Benedict, of Charles de Foucauld or the brothers of Taizé. For them solitude is not a private therapeutic place. Rather, it is the place of conversion, the place where the old self dies and the new self is born, the place where the emergence of the new man and the new woman occurs.

How can we gain a clearer understanding of this transforming solitude? Let me try to describe in more detail the struggle as well as the encounter that takes place in this solitude.

In solitude I get rid of my scaffolding: no friends to talk with, no telephone calls to make, no meetings to attend, no music to entertain, no books to distract, just me – naked, vulnerable, weak, sinful, deprived, broken – nothing. It is this nothingness that I have to face in my solitude, a nothingness so dreadful that everything in me wants to run to my friends, my work, and my distractions so that I can forget my nothingness and make myself believe that I am worth something. But that is not all. As soon as I decide to stay in my solitude, confusing ideas, disturbing images, wild fantasies, and weird associations jump about in my mind like monkeys in a banana tree. Anger and greed begin to show their ugly faces. I give long, hostile speeches to my enemies and dream lustful dreams in which I am wealthy, influential, and very attractive – or poor, ugly, and in need of immediate consolation. Thus I try again to run from the dark abyss of my nothingness and restore my false self in all its vainglory.

The task is to persevere in my solitude, to stay in my cell until all my seductive visitors get tired of pounding on my door and leave me alone. The 'Isenheim Altar' painted by Grünewald shows with frightening realism the ugly faces of the many demons who tempted Anthony in his solitude. The struggle is real because the danger is real. It is the danger of living the whole of our life as one long defense against the reality of our condition, one restless effort to convince ourselves of our virtuousness. Yet Jesus 'did not come to call the virtuous, but sinners' (Matthew 9:13).

That is the struggle. It is the struggle to die to the false self. But this struggle is far, far beyond our own strength. Anyone who wants to fight his demons with his own weapons is a fool. The wisdom of the desert is that the confrontation with our own frightening nothingness forces us to surrender ourselves totally and unconditionally to the Lord Jesus Christ. Alone, we cannot face 'the mystery of iniquity' with impunity. Only Christ can overcome the powers of evil. Only in and through him can we survive the trials of our solitude. This is beautifully illustrated by Abba Elias, who said: 'An old man was living in a temple and the demons came to say to him, "Leave this place which belongs to us," and the old man said, "No place belongs to you." Then they began to scatter his palm leaves about, one by one, and the old man went on gathering them together with persistence. A little later the devil took his hand and pulled him to the door. When the old man reached the door, he seized the lintel with the other hand crying out, "Jesus, save me." Immediately the devil fled away. Then the old man began to weep. Then the Lord said to him, "Why are you weeping?" and the old man said, "Because the devils have dared to seize a man and treat him like this." The Lord said to him, "You had been careless. As soon as you turned to me again, you see I was beside you." '[2] This story shows that only in the context of the great encounter with Jesus Christ himself can a real authentic struggle take place. The encounter with Christ does not take place before, after, or beyond the struggle with our false self and its demons. No, it is precisely in the midst of this struggle that our Lord comes to us and says, as he said to the old man in the story: 'As soon as you turned to me again, you see I was beside you.'

We enter into solitude first of all to meet our Lord and to be with him and him alone. Our primary task in solitude, therefore, is not to pay undue attention to the many faces which assail us, but to keep the eyes of our mind and heart on him who is our divine savior. Only in the context of grace can we face our sin; only in the place of healing do we dare to show our wounds; only with a single-minded attention to Christ can we give up our clinging fears and face our own true nature. As we come to realize that it is not we who live, but Christ who lives in us, that he is our true self, we can slowly let our compulsions melt away and begin to experience the freedom of the children of God. And then we can look back with a smile and realize that we aren't even angry or greedy any more.

What does all of this mean for us in our daily life? Even when we are not called to the monastic life, or do not have the physical constitution to survive the rigors of the desert, we are still responsible for our own solitude. Precisely because our secular milieu offers us so few spiritual disciplines, we have to develop our own. We have, indeed, to fashion our own desert where we can withdraw every day, shake off our compulsions, and dwell in the gentle healing presence of our Lord. Without such a desert we will lose our own soul while preaching the gospel to others. But with such a spiritual abode, we will become increasingly conformed to him in whose Name we minister.

The very first thing we need to do is set apart a time and a place to be with God and him alone. The concrete shape of this discipline of solitude will be different for each person depending on individual character, ministerial task, and milieu. But a real discipline never remains vague or general. It is as concrete and specific as daily life itself. When I visited Mother Teresa of Calcutta a few years ago and asked her how to live out my vocation as a priest, she simply said: 'Spend one hour a day in adoration of your Lord and never do anything you know is wrong, and you will be all right.' She might have said something else to a married person with young children and something else again to someone who lives in a larger community. But like all great disciples of Jesus, Mother Teresa affirmed again the truth that ministry can be fruitful only if it grows out of a direct and intimate encounter with our Lord. Thus the opening words of St. John's first letter echo down through history: 'Something . . . we have heard, and we have seen with our own eyes; that we have watched and touched with our hands: the Word, who is life – this is our subject' (1 John 1:1).

Solitude is thus the place of purification and transformation, the place of the great struggle and the great encounter. Solitude is not simply a means to an end.

Solitude is its own end. It is the place where Christ remodels us in his own image and frees us from the victimizing compulsions of the world. Solitude is the place of our salvation. Hence, it is the place where we want to lead all who are seeking the light in this dark world. St. Anthony spent twenty years in isolation. When he left it he took his solitude with him and shared it with all who came to him. Those who saw him described him as balanced, gentle, and caring. He had become so Christlike, so radiant with God's love, that his entire being was ministry.

Let me now try to show how a compassionate ministry flows from a transformed self.

A Compassionate Ministry

Anthony's life after he had emerged from his period of total isolation was blessed by a rich and varied ministry. People from many walks of life came to him and asked for advice. The solitude that at first had required physical isolation had now become a quality of his heart, an inner disposition that could no longer be disturbed by those who needed his guidance. Somehow his solitude had become an infinite space into which anyone could be invited. His advice was simple, direct, and concrete: 'Someone asked him: "What must one do in order to please God?" The old man replied, "Pay attention to what I tell you: whoever you may be, always have God before your eyes; whatever you do, do it according to the testimony of the holy Scriptures; in whatever place you live, do not easily leave it. Keep these three precepts and you will be saved." '[3]

To Abba Pambo, who asked him, 'What ought I to do?' the old man said: 'Do not trust in your own righteousness, do not worry about the past, but control your tongue and your stomach.' And looking into the future, Anthony said with words which have an eerie timeliness: 'A time is coming when men will go mad, and when they see someone who is not mad, they will attack him saying, "You are mad, you are not like us." '[4] Through the struggle with his demons and the encounter with his Lord, Anthony had learned to diagnose the hearts of people and the mood of his time and thus to offer insight, comfort, and consolation. Solitude had made him a compassionate man.

Here we reach the point where ministry and spirituality touch each other. It is compassion. Compassion is the fruit of solitude and the basis of all ministry. The purification and transformation that take place in solitude manifest themselves in compassion.

Let us not underestimate how hard it is to be compassionate. Compassion is hard because it requires the inner disposition to go with others to the place where they are weak, vulnerable, lonely, and broken. But this is not our spontaneous response to suffering. What we desire most is to do away with suffering by fleeing from it or finding a quick cure for it. As busy, active, relevant ministers, we want to earn our bread by making a real contribution. This means first and foremost doing something to show that our presence makes a difference. And so we ignore our greatest gift, which is our ability to enter into solidarity with those who suffer.

It is in solitude that this compassionate solidarity grows. In solitude we realize that nothing human is alien to us, that the roots of all conflict, war, injustice, cruelty, hatred, jealousy, and envy are deeply anchored in our own heart. In solitude our heart of stone can be turned into a heart of flesh, a rebellious heart into a contrite heart, and a closed heart into a heart that can open itself to all suffering people in a gesture of solidarity.

If you would ask the Desert Fathers why solitude gives birth to compassion, they would say, 'Because it makes us die to our neighbor.' At first this answer seems quite disturbing to a modern mind. But when we give it a closer look we can see that in order to be of service to others we have to die to them; that is, we have to give up measuring our meaning and value with the yardstick of others. To die to our neighbors means to stop judging them, to stop evaluating them, and thus to become free to be compassionate.

Compassion can never coexist with judgment because judgment creates the distance, the distinction, which prevents us from really being with the other.

Much of our ministry is pervaded with judgments. Often quite unconsciously we classify our people as very good, good, neutral, bad, and very bad. These judgments influence deeply the thoughts, words, and actions of our ministry. Before we know it, we fall into the trap of the self-fulfilling prophecy. Those whom we consider lazy, indifferent, hostile, or obnoxious we treat as such, forcing them in this way to live up to our own views. And so, much of our ministry is limited by the snares of our own judgments. These self-created limits prevent us from being available to people and shrivel up our compassion.

'Do not judge and you will not be judged yourselves' is a word of Jesus that is indeed very hard to live up to. But it contains the secret of a compassionate ministry. This becomes clear in many stories from the desert. Abba Moses, one of St. Anthony's followers, said to a brother: 'To die to one's neighbor is this. To bear your own faults and not to pay attention to anyone else wondering whether they are good or bad. Do no harm to anyone, do not think anything bad in your heart towards anyone, do not scorn the man who does evil, do not put confidence in him who does wrong to his neighbor, do not rejoice with him who injures his neighbor . . . Do not have hostile feelings towards anyone and do not let dislike dominate your heart.'[5] And with the typically graphic imagery of the desert, everything is summarized with the words: 'It is folly for a man who has a dead person in his house to leave him there and go to weep over his neighbor's dead.'[6]

Solitude leads to the awareness of the dead person in our own house and keeps us from making judgments about other people's sins. In this way real forgiveness becomes possible. The following desert story offers a good illustration: 'A brother . . . committed a fault. A council was called to which Abba Moses was invited, but he refused to go to it. Then the priest sent someone to say to him, "Come, for everyone is waiting for you." So he got up and went. He took a leaking jug, filled it with water, and carried it with him. The others came out to meet him and said to him, "What is this, Father?" The old man said to them, "My sins run out behind me, and I do not see them, and today I am coming to judge the error of another." When they heard that they said no more to the brother but forgave him.'[7]

What becomes visible here is that solitude molds self-righteous people into gentle, caring, forgiving persons who are so deeply convinced of their own great sinfulness and so fully aware of God's even greater mercy that their life itself becomes ministry. In such a ministry there is hardly any difference left between doing and being. When we are filled with

God's merciful presence, we can do nothing other than minister because our whole being witnesses to the light that has come into the darkness. Here are two desert stories that show this tender, compassionate ministry.

'Of Abba Ammonas, a disciple of Anthony, it is said that in his solitude he "advanced to the point where his goodness was so great that he took no notice of wickedness." Thus, having become bishop, someone brought a young girl who was pregnant to him, saying, "See what this unhappy wretch has done; give her a penance." But he, having marked the young girl's womb with the sign of the cross, commanded that six pairs of fine linen sheets should be given her, saying, "It is for fear that, when she comes to give birth, she may die, she or the child, and have nothing for the burial." But her accusers resumed, "Why did you do that? Give her a punishment." But he said to them, "Look, brothers, she is near to death; what am I to do?" Then he sent her away and no old man dared accuse anyone any more.'[8]

This story illustrates beautifully how the compassionate person is so aware of the suffering of others that it is not even possible for him or her to dwell on their sins. The second story makes clear how extremely careful and sensitive is a compassionate minister.

'Three old men, of whom one had a bad reputation, came one day to Abba Achilles. The first asked him, "Father, make me a fishing-net." "I will not make you one," he replied. Then the second said, "Of your charity make one, so that we have a souvenir of you in the monastery." But he said, "I do not have time." Then the third one, who had a bad reputation, said, "Make me a fishing-net, so that I may have something from your hands, Father." Abba Achilles answered him at once, "For you, I will make one." Then the two other old men asked him privately, "Why did you not want to do what we asked you, but you promised to do what he asked?" The old man gave them this answer, "I told you I would not make one, and you were not disappointed, since you thought that I had no time. But if I had not made one for him, he would have said, "The old man has heard about my sin, and that is why he does not want to make me anything," and so our relationship would have broken down. But now I have cheered his soul, so that he will not be overcome with grief." "[9]

Here indeed is ministry in its purest form, a compassionate ministry born of solitude. Anthony and his followers, who escaped the compulsions of the world, did so not out of disdain for people but in order to be able to save them. Thomas Merton, who described these monks as people who swam for their life in order not to drown in the sinking ship of their society, remarks:

> They knew that they were helpless to do any good for

> others as long as they floundered about in the wreckage. But once they got a foothold on solid ground, things were different. Then they had not only the power but even the obligation to pull the whole world to safety after them."[10]

Thus in and through solitude we do not move away from people. On the contrary, we move closer to them through compassionate ministry.

Conclusion

In a world that victimizes us by its compulsions, we are called to solitude where we can struggle against our anger and greed and let our new self be born in the loving encounter with Jesus Christ. It is in this solitude that we become compassionate people, deeply aware of our solidarity in brokenness with all of humanity and ready to reach out to anyone in need.

The end of Anthony's story shows him, after years of compassionate ministry, returning to his solitude to be totally absorbed in direct communion with God. One of the desert stories tells us about a certain old man who asked God to let him see the Fathers. God heard his prayer and the old man saw them all except Anthony. 'So he asked his guide, "Where is Abba Anthony?" He told him in reply that in the place where God is, there Anthony would be.'[11] It is very important for us to realize that Anthony concluded his life in total absorption in God. The goal of our life is not people. It is God. Only in him shall we find the rest we seek. It is therefore to solitude that we must return, not alone, but with all those whom we embrace through our ministry. This return continues until the time when the same Lord who sent us into the world calls us back to be with him in a never-ending communion.

Silence

Introduction

When Arsenius, the Roman educator who exchanged his status and wealth for the solitude of the Egyptian desert, prayed, 'Lord, lead me into the way of salvation,' he heard a voice saying, 'Be silent.' Silence completes and intensifies solitude. This is the conviction shared by the Desert Fathers. A charming story about Abbot Macarius makes the point quite well. 'Once the abbot Macarius, after he had given the benediction to the brethren in the church at Scete, said to them, "Brethren, fly." One of the elders answered him, "How can we fly further than this, seeing we are here in the desert?" Then Macarius placed his finger on his mouth and said, "Fly from this." So saying, he entered his cell and shut the door.'[1]

Silence is the way to make solitude a reality. The Desert Fathers praise silence as the safest way to God. 'I have often repented of having spoken,' Arsenius said, 'but never of having remained silent.' One day Archbishop Theophilus came to the desert to visit Abba Pambo. But Abba Pambo did not speak to him. When the brethren finally said to Pambo, 'Father, say something to the archbishop, so that he may be edified,' he replied: 'If he is not edified by my silence, he will not be edified by my speech.'[2]

Silence is an indispensable discipline in the spiritual life. Ever since James described the tongue as a 'whole wicked world in itself' and silence as putting a bit into the horse's mouth (James 3:3, 6) Christians have tried to practice silence as the way to self-control. Clearly silence is a discipline needed in many different situations: in teaching and learning, in preaching and worship, in visiting and counseling. Silence is a very concrete, practical, and useful discipline in all our ministerial tasks. It can be seen as a portable cell taken with us from the solitary place into the midst of our ministry. Silence is solitude practiced in action.

In this reflection I would like first to show how wordy our world has become. Then I want to describe the great value of silence in this wordy world. Finally I hope to indicate how silence can be a sign of God's presence in the different forms of ministry.

Our Wordy World

Over the last few decades we have been inundated by a torrent of words. Wherever we go we are surrounded by words: words softly whispered, loudly proclaimed, or angrily screamed; words spoken, recited, or sung; words on records, in books, on walls, or in the sky; words in many sounds, many colors, or many forms; words to be heard, read, seen, or glanced at; words which flicker off and on, move slowly, dance, jump, or wiggle. Words, words, words! They form the floor, the walls, and the ceiling of our existence.

It has not always been this way. There was a time not too long ago without radios and televisions, stop signs, yield signs, merge signs, bumper stickers, and the ever-present announcements indicating price increases or special sales. There was a time without the advertisements which now cover whole cities with words.

Recently I was driving through Los Angeles, and suddenly I had the strange sensation of driving through a huge dictionary. Wherever I looked there were words trying to take my eyes from the road. They said, 'Use me, take me, buy me, drink me, smell me, touch me, kiss me, sleep with me.' In such a world who can maintain respect for words?

All this is to suggest that words, my own included, have lost their creative power. Their limitless multiplication has made us lose confidence in words and caused us to think, more often than not, 'They are just words.'

Teachers speak to students for six, twelve, eighteen, and sometimes twenty-four years. But the students often emerge from the experience with the feeling,

'They were just words.' Preachers preach their sermons week after week and year after year. But their parishioners remain the same and often think, 'They are just words.' Politicians, businessmen, ayatollahs, and popes give speeches and make statements 'in season and out of season,' but those who listen say: 'They are just words . . . just another distraction.'

The result of this is that the main function of the word, which is communication, is no longer realized. The word no longer communicates, no longer fosters communion, no longer creates community, and therefore no longer gives life. The word no longer offers trustworthy ground on which people can meet each other other and build society.

Do I exaggerate? Let us focus for a moment on theological education. What else is the goal of theological education than to bring us closer to the Lord our God so that we may be more faithful to the great commandment to love him with all our heart, with all our soul, and with all our mind, and our neighbor as ourselves (Matthew 22:37)? Seminaries and divinity schools must lead theology students into an ever-growing communion with God, with each other, and with their fellow human beings. Theological education is meant to form our whole person toward an increasing conformity with the mind of Christ so that our way of praying and our way of believing will be one.

But is this what takes place? Often it seems that we who study or teach theology find ourselves entangled in such a complex network of discussions, debates, and arguments about God and 'God-issues' that a simple conversation with God or a simple presence to God has become practically impossible. Our heightened verbal ability, which enables us to make many distinctions, has sometimes become a poor substitute for a single-minded commitment to the Word who is life. If there is a crisis in theological education, it is first and foremost a crisis of the word. This is not to say that critical intellectual work and the subtle distinctions it requires have no place in theological training. But when our words are no longer a reflection of the divine Word in and through whom the world has been created and redeemed, they lose their grounding and become as seductive and misleading as the words used to sell Geritol.

There was a time when the obvious milieu for theological education was the monastery. There words were born out of silence and could lead one deeper into silence. Although monasteries are no longer the most common places of theological education, silence remains as indispensable today as it was in the past. The Word of God is born out of the eternal silence of God, and it is to this Word out of silence that we want to be witnesses.

Silence

Silence is the home of the word. Silence gives strength and fruitfulness to the word. We can even say that words are meant to disclose the mystery of the silence from which they come.

The Taoist philosopher Chuang Tzu expresses this well in the following way:

> The purpose of a fish trap is to catch fish and when the fish are caught, the trap is forgotten. The purpose of a rabbit snare is to catch rabbits. When the rabbits are caught, the snare is forgotten. The purpose of the word is to convey ideas. When the ideas are grasped, the words are forgotten. Where can I find a man who has forgotten words? He is the one I would like to talk to.[3]

'I would like to talk to the man who has forgotten words.' That could have been said by one of the Desert Fathers. For them, the word is the instrument of the present world and silence is the mystery of the future world. If a word is to bear fruit it must be spoken from the future world into the present world. The Desert Fathers therefore considered their going into the silence of the desert to be a first step into the future world. From that world their words could bear fruit, because there they could be filled with the power of God's silence.

In the sayings of the Desert Fathers, we can distinguish three aspects of silence. All of them deepen and strengthen the central idea that silence is the mystery of the future world. First, silence makes us pilgrims. Secondly, silence guards the fire within. Thirdly, silence teaches us to speak.

Silence Makes Us Pilgrims

Abba Tithoes once said, 'Pilgrimage means that a man should control his tongue.' The expression 'To be on pilgrimage is to be silent' (*peregrinatio est tacere*), expresses the conviction of the Desert Fathers that silence is the best anticipation of the future world.[4] The most frequent argument for silence is simply that words lead to sin. Not speaking, therefore, is the most obvious way to stay away from sin. This connection is clearly expressed by the apostle James: '. . . every one of us does something wrong, over and over again; the only man who could reach perfection would be someone who never said anything wrong – he would be able to control every part of himself' (James 3:2).

James leaves little doubt that speaking without sinning is very difficult and that, if we want to remain untouched by the sins of the world on our journey to our eternal home, silence is the safest way. Thus, silence became one of the central disciplines of the spiritual life. St. Benedict, the father of the monastic life in the West and the patron saint of Europe, puts great emphasis on silence in his Rule. He quotes the Psalmist who says, 'I will keep a muzzle on my mouth . . . I will watch how I behave and not let my tongue lead me into sin' (Psalm 39:1). St. Benedict not only warns his brothers against evil talk, but also tells them to avoid good, holy, edifying words because, as it is written in the book of Proverbs, 'A flood of words is never without its faults' (Proverbs 10:19). Speaking is dangerous and easily leads us away from the right path.

The central idea underlying these ascetic teachings is that speaking gets us involved in the affairs of the world, and it is very hard to be involved without becoming entangled in and polluted by the world. The Desert Fathers and all who followed in their footsteps, 'knew that every conversation tended to interest them in this world, to make them in heart less of strangers here and more of citizens.'[5]

This might sound too unworldly to us, but let us at least recognize how often we come out of a conversation, a discussion, a social gathering, or a business meeting with a bad taste in our mouth. How seldom have long talks proved to be good and fruitful? Would not many if not most of the words we use be better left unspoken? We speak about the events of the world, but how often do we really change them for the better? We speak about people and their ways, but how often do our words do them or us any good? We speak about our ideas and feelings as if everyone were interested in them, but how often do we really feel understood? We speak a great deal about God and religion, but how often does it bring us or others real insight? Words often leave us with a sense of inner defeat. They can even create a sense of numbness and a feeling of being bogged down in swampy ground. Often they leave us in a slight depression, or in a fog that clouds the window of our mind. In short, words can give us the feeling of having stopped too long at one of the little villages that we pass on our journey, of having been motivated more by curiosity than by service. Words often make us forget that we are pilgrims called to invite others to join us on the journey. *Peregrinatio est tacere*. 'To be silent keeps us pilgrims.'

Silence Guards The Fire Within

A second, more positive, meaning of silence is that it protects the inner fire. Silence guards the inner heat of religious emotions. This inner heat is the life of the Holy Spirit within us. Thus, silence is the discipline by which the inner fire of God is tended and kept alive.

Diadochus of Photiki offers us a very concrete image: 'When the door of the steambath is continually left open, the heat inside rapidly escapes through it;

likewise the soul, in its desire to say many things, dissipates its remembrance of God through the door of speech, even though everything it says may be good. Thereafter the intellect, though lacking appropriate ideas, pours out a welter of confused thoughts to anyone it meets, as it no longer has the Holy Spirit to keep its understanding free from fantasy. Ideas of value always shun verbosity, being foreign to confusion and fantasy. Timely silence, then, is precious, for it is nothing less than the mother of the wisest thoughts.'[6]

These words of Diadochus go against the grain of our contemporary life-style, in which 'sharing' has become one of the greatest virtues. We have been made to believe that feelings, emotions, and even the inner stirrings of our soul have to be shared with others. Expressions such as 'Thanks for sharing this with me,' or 'It was good to share this with you,' show that the door of our steambath is open most of the time. In fact, people who prefer to keep to themselves and do not expose their interior life tend to create uneasiness and are often considered inhibited, asocial, or simply odd. But let us at least raise the question of whether our lavish ways of sharing are not more compulsive than virtuous; that instead of creating community they tend to flatten out our life together. Often we come home from a sharing session with a feeling that something precious has been taken away from us or that holy ground has been trodden upon. James

Hannay, commenting on the sayings of the Desert Fathers, writes:

> The mouth is not a door through which any evil enters. The ears are such doors as are the eyes. The mouth is a door only for exit. What was it that they [the Desert Fathers] feared to let go out? What was it which someone might steal out of their hearts, as a thief takes the steed from the stable when the door is left open? It can have been nothing else than the force of religious emotion.[7]

What needs to be guarded is the life of the Spirit within us. Especially we who want to witness to the presence of God's Spirit in the world need to tend the fire within with utmost care. It is not so strange that many ministers have become burnt-out cases, people who say many words and share many experiences, but in whom the fire of God's Spirit has died and from whom not much more comes forth than their own boring, petty ideas and feelings. Sometimes it seems that our many words are more an expression of our doubt than of our faith. It is as if we are not sure that God's Spirit can touch the hearts of people: we have to help him out and, with many words, convince others of his power. But it is precisely this wordy unbelief that quenches the fire.

Our first and foremost task is faithfully to care for the inward fire so that when it is really needed it can offer warmth and light to lost travelers. Nobody expressed this with more conviction than the Dutch painter Vincent van Gogh:

> There may be a great fire in our soul, yet no one ever comes to warm himself at it, and the passersby only see a wisp of smoke coming through the chimney, and go along their way. Look here, now what must be done? Must one tend the inner fire, have salt in oneself, wait patiently yet with how much impatience for the hour when somebody will come and sit down – maybe to stay? Let him who believes in God wait for the hour that will come sooner or later.[8]

Vincent van Gogh speaks here with the mind and heart of the Desert Fathers. He knew about the temptation to open all the doors so that passersby could see the fire and not just the smoke coming through the chimney. But he also realized that if this happened, the fire would die and nobody would find warmth and new strength. His own life is a powerful example of faithfulness to the inner fire. During his life nobody came to sit down at his fire, but today thousands have found comfort and consolation in his drawings, paintings, and letters.

As ministers our greatest temptation is toward too many words. They weaken our faith and make us lukewarm. But silence is a sacred discipline, a guard of the Holy Spirit.

Silence Teaches Us To Speak

The third way that silence reveals itself as the mystery of the future world is by teaching us to speak. A word with power is a word that comes out of silence. A word that bears fruit is a word that emerges from the silence and returns to it. It is a word that reminds us of the silence from which it comes and leads us back to that silence. A word that is not rooted in silence is a weak, powerless word that sounds like a 'clashing cymbal or a booming gong' (1 Corinthians 13:1).

All this is true only when the silence from which the word comes forth is not emptiness and absence, but fullness and presence, not the human silence of embarrassment, shame, or guilt, but the divine silence in which love rests secure.

Here we can glimpse the great mystery in which we participate through silence and the Word, the mystery of God's own speaking. Out of his eternal silence God spoke the Word, and through this Word created and recreated the world. In the beginning God spoke the land, the sea, and the sky. He spoke the sun, the moon, and the stars. He spoke plants, birds, fish, animals wild and tame. Finally, he spoke man and woman. Then, in the fullness of time, God's Word, through whom all had been created, became flesh and gave power to all who believe to become the children of God. In all this, the Word of God does not break the silence of God, but rather unfolds the immeasurable richness of his silence.

By entering into the Egyptian desert, the monks wanted to participate in the divine silence. By speaking out of this silence to the needs of their people, they sought to participate in the creative and recreative power of the divine Word.

Words can only create communion and thus new life when they embody the silence from which they emerge. As soon as we begin to take hold of each other by our words, and use words to defend ourselves or offend others, the word no longer speaks of silence. But when the word calls forth the healing and restoring stillness of its own silence, few words are needed: much can be said without much being spoken.

Thus silence is the mystery of the future world. It keeps us pilgrims and prevents us from becoming entangled in the cares of this age. It guards the fire of the Holy Spirit who dwells within us. It allows us to speak a word that participates in the creative and recreative power of God's own Word.

The Ministry of Silence

We are now left with the question of how to practice a ministry of silence in which our word has the power to represent the fullness of God's silence. This is an important question because we have become so contaminated by our wordy world that we hold to the deceptive opinion that our words are more important than our silence. Therefore it requires a strenuous discipline to make our ministry one that leads our people into the silence of God. That is the task Jesus has given us. The whole of Jesus' ministry pointed away from himself to the Father who had sent him. To his disciples Jesus said, 'The words I say to you I do not speak as from myself; it is the Father, living in me, who is doing this work' (John 14:10). Jesus, the Word of God made flesh, spoke not to attract attention to himself but to show the way to his Father: 'I came from the Father and have come into the world and now I leave the world to go to the Father (John 16:28). I am going to prepare a place for you . . . so that where I am you may be too' (John 14:2–3). In order to be a ministry in the Name of Jesus, our ministry must also point beyond our words to the unspeakable mystery of God.

One of our main problems is that in this chatty society, silence has become a very fearful thing. For most people, silence creates itchiness and nervousness. Many experience silence not as full and rich, but as empty and hollow. For them silence is like a gaping abyss which can swallow them up. As soon as a minister says during a worship service, 'Let us be silent for a few moments,' people tend to become restless and preoccupied with only one thought: 'When will this be over?' Imposed silence often creates hostility and resentment. Many ministers who have experimented with silence in their services have soon found out that silence can be more demonic than divine and have quickly picked up the signals that were saying: 'Please keep talking.' It is quite understandable that most forms of ministry avoid silence precisely so as to ward off the anxiety it provokes.

But isn't the purpose of all ministry to reveal that God is not a God of fear but a God of love? And couldn't this be accomplished by gently and carefully converting the empty silence into a full silence, the anxious silence into a peaceful silence, and the restless silence into a restful silence, so that in this converted silence a real encounter with the loving Father could take place? What a power our word would have if it could enable people to befriend their silence! Let me describe a few concrete ways in which this might happen.

Silence and Preaching

Our preaching, when it is good, is interesting or moving, and sometimes both. It stimulates mind and heart and thus leads to a new insight or a new feeling. This is both valuable and necessary. But there is another option, one which is especially appropriate when we work with small groups. There is a way of preaching in which the word of Scripture is repeated quietly and regularly, with a short comment here and there, in order to let that word create an inner space where we can listen to our Lord. If it is true that the word of Scripture should lead us into the silence of God, then we must be careful to use that word not simply as an interesting or motivating word, but as a word that creates the boundaries within which we can listen to the loving, caring, gentle presence of God.

Most people who listen to a sermon keep their eyes directed toward the preacher, and rightly so, because he or she asks for attention to the word that is being spoken. But is it also possible for the word to be spoken in such a way that it slowly moves attention away from the pulpit to the heart of the listener and reveals there an inner silence in which it is safe to dwell.

The simple words 'The Lord is my shepherd' can be spoken quietly and persistently in such a way that they become like a hedge around a garden in which God's shepherding can be sensed. These words, which at first might seem to be no more than an interesting metaphor, can slowly descend from the mind into the heart. There they may offer the context in which an inner transformation, by the God who transcends all human words and concepts, can take place. Thus, the words 'The Lord is my shepherd' lead to the silent pastures where we can dwell in the loving presence of him in whose Name the preacher speaks. This meditative preaching is one way to practice the ministry of silence.

Silence and Counseling

Counseling is understood by many to be a way in which one person listens to another and guides him or her to better self-understanding and greater emotional independence. But it is also possible to experience the relationship between pastor and counselee as a way of entering together into the loving silence of God and waiting there for the healing Word. The Holy Spirit is called the divine Counselor. He is actively present in the lives of those who come together to discern God's will. This is why human counselors should see as their primary task the work of helping their parishioners to become aware of the movements of the divine Counselor and encouraging them to follow these movements without fear. In this perspective, pastoral counseling is the attempt to lead fearful parishioners into the silence of God, and to help them feel at home there, trusting that they will slowly discover the healing presence of the Spirit.

This suggests that the human counselor needs to be very sensitive to the words of Scripture as words emerging from God's silence and directed to specific people in specific circumstances. When a word from

Scripture is spoken by a counselor at that particular moment when the parishioner is able to hear it, it can indeed shatter huge walls of fear and open up unexpected perspectives. Such a word then brings with it the divine silence from which it came and to which it returns.

Silence and Organizing

Finally, I would like to stress the importance of silence in the ways a minister organizes his own life and that of others. In a society in which entertainment and distraction are such important preoccupations, ministers are also tempted to join the ranks of those who consider it their primary task to keep other people busy. It is easy to perceive the young and the elderly as people who need to be kept off the streets or on the streets. And ministers frequently find themselves in fierce competition with people and institutions who offer something more exciting to do than they do.

But our task is the opposite of distraction. Our task is to help people concentrate on the real but often hidden event of God's active presence in their lives. Hence, the question that must guide all organizing activity in a parish is not how to keep people busy, but how to keep them from being so busy that they can no longer hear the voice of God who speaks in silence.

Calling people together, therefore, means calling them away from the fragmenting and distracting wordiness of the dark world to that silence in which they can discover themselves, each other, and God. Thus organizing can be seen as the creation of a space where communion becomes possible and community can develop.

These examples of silence in preaching, counseling, and organizing are meant to illustrate how silence can help to determine the practical shape of our ministry. But let us not be too literal about silence. After all, silence of the heart is much more important than silence of the mouth. Abba Poemen said: 'A man may seem to be silent, but if his heart is condemning others he is babbling ceaselessly. But there may be another who talks from morning till night and yet he is truly silent.'[9]

Silence is primarily a quality of the heart that leads to ever-growing charity. Once a visitor said to a hermit, 'Sorry for making you break your rule.' But the monk answered: 'My rule is to practice the virtue of hospitality towards those who come to see me and send them home in peace.'[10]

Charity, not silence, is the purpose of the spiritual life and of ministry. About this all the Desert Fathers are unanimous.

Conclusion

This brings me to the end of my reflection on silence. In our chatty world, in which the word has lost its power to communicate, silence helps us to keep our mind and heart anchored in the future world and allows us to speak from there a creative and recreative word to the present world. Thus silence can also give us concrete guidance in the practice of our ministry.

There is little doubt that the Desert Fathers believed that simply not speaking is a very important practice. Too often our words are superfluous, inauthentic, and shallow. It is a good discipline to wonder in each new situation if people wouldn't be better served by our silence than by our words. But having acknowledged this, a more important message from the desert is that silence is above all a quality of the heart that can stay with us even in our conversation with others. It is a portable cell that we carry with us wherever we go. From it we speak to those in need and to it we return after our words have born fruit.

It is in this portable cell that we find ourselves immersed in the divine silence. The final question concerning our ministry of silence is not whether we say much or little, but whether our words call forth the caring silence of God himself. It is to this silence that we all are called: words are the instrument of the present world, but silence is the mystery of the future world.

Prayer

Introduction

When Arsenius had asked for the second time, 'Lord, lead me to the way of salvation,' the voice that spoke to him not only said, 'Be silent' but also, 'Pray always.' To pray always – this is the real purpose of the desert life. Solitude and silence can never be separated from the call to unceasing prayer. If solitude were primarily an escape from a busy job, and silence primarily an escape from a noisy milieu, they could easily become very self-centered forms of asceticism. But solitude and silence are for prayer. The Desert Fathers did not think of solitude as being alone, but as being alone with God. They did not think of silence as not speaking, but as listening to God. Solitude and silence are the context within which prayer is practiced.

The literal translation of the words 'pray always' is 'come to rest.' The Greek word for rest is *hesychia*, and hesychasm is the term which refers to the spirituality of the desert. A hesychast is a man or a woman who seeks solitude and silence as the ways to unceasing prayer. The prayer of the hesychasts is a prayer of rest.

This rest, however, has little to do with the absence of conflict or pain. It is a rest in God in the midst of a very intense daily struggle. Abba Anthony even says to a fellow monk that it belongs 'to the great work of a man . . . to expect temptations to his last breath.' *Hesychia*, the rest which flows from unceasing prayer, needs to be sought at all costs, even when the flesh is itchy, the world alluring, and the demons noisy. Mother Theodora, one of the Desert Mothers, makes this very clear: ' . . . you should realize that as soon as you intend to live in peace, at once evil comes and weighs down your soul through *accidie* [sense of boredom], faintheartedness, and evil thoughts. It also attacks your body through sickness, debility, weakening of the knees, and all the members. It dissipates the strength of soul and body, so that one believes one is ill and no longer able to pray. But if we are vigilant, all these temptations fall away.'[1]

Although weakness of the knees is not likely to be our main complaint, we ministers have no lack of excuses, often very sophisticated ones, for staying away from prayer. For us, however, prayer is as important as it was for the early Desert Fathers. Let me therefore explore the role of prayer in our daily lives. I will first express my suspicion that we tend to see prayer primarily as an activity of the mind. Then I would like to present the prayer of the hesychasts as a prayer of the heart. Finally, I want to show how this prayer of the heart calls for a discipline in order to make it the center of our daily ministry.

The Prayer of the Mind

Very few ministers will deny that prayer is important. They will not even deny that prayer is the most important dimension of their lives. But the fact is that most ministers pray very little or not at all. They realize that they should not forget to pray, that they should take time to pray, and that prayer should be a priority in their lives. But all these 'shoulds' do not have the power to carry them over the enormous obstacle of their activism. There is always one more phone call, one more letter, one more visit, one more meeting, one more book, and one more party. Together these form an insurmountable pile of activities. The contrast between the great support for the idea of prayer and the lack of support for the practice of it is so blatantly visible that it becomes quite easy to believe in the ruses of the evil one which Amma Theodora described in such vivid detail.

One of these demonic ruses is to make us think of prayer primarily as an activity of the mind that involves above all else our intellectual capacities. This prejudice reduces prayer to speaking with God or thinking about God.

For many of us prayer means nothing more than speaking with God. And since it usually seems to be a quite one-sided affair, prayer simply means talking to God. This idea is enough to create great frustrations. If I present a problem, I expect a solution; if I formulate a question, I expect an answer; if I ask for guidance, I expect a response. And when it seems, increasingly, that I am talking into the dark, it is not so strange that I soon begin to suspect that my dialogue with God is in fact a monologue. Then I may begin to ask myself: To whom am I really speaking, God or myself?

Sometimes the absence of an answer makes us wonder if we might have said the wrong kind of prayers, but mostly we feel taken, cheated, and quickly stop 'this whole silly thing.' It is quite understandable that we should experience speaking with real people, who need a word and who offer a response, as much more meaningful than speaking with a God who seems to be an expert at hide-and-seek.

But there is another viewpoint that can lead to similar frustrations. This is the viewpoint that restricts the meaning of prayer to thinking about God. Whether we call this prayer or meditation makes little difference. The basic conviction is that what is needed is to think thoughts about God and his mysteries. Prayer therefore requires hard mental work and is quite fatiguing, especially if reflective thinking is not one of our strengths. Since we already have so many other practical and pressing things on our minds, thinking about God becomes one more demanding burden. This is especially true because thinking about God is not a spontaneous event, while thinking about pressing concerns comes quite naturally.

Thinking about God makes God into a subject that needs to be scrutinized or analyzed. Successful prayer is thus prayer that leads to new intellectual discoveries about God. Just as a psychologist studies a case and seeks to gain insight by trying to find coherence in all the available data, so someone who prays well should come to understand God better by thinking deeply about all that is known about him.

In thinking about God, as with speaking to God, our frustration tolerance is quite low, and it does not take much to stop praying altogether. Reading a book or writing an article or sermon is a lot more satisfying than this mental wandering into the unknown.

Both these views of prayer are the products of a culture in which high value is placed on mastering the world through the intellect. The dominating idea has been that everything can be understood and that what can be understood can be controlled. God, too, is a problem that has a solution, and by strenuous efforts of the mind we will find it. It is therefore not so strange that the academic gown is the official garb of the minister, and that one of the main criteria for admission to the pulpit is a university degree.

This, of course, does not mean that the intellect has no place in the life of prayer, or that theological reflection and prayer are mutually exclusive. But we should not underestimate the intellectualism of the mainstream North American churches. If the public prayers of ministers inside as well as outside of church buildings are any indication of their prayer life, God is certainly busy attending seminars. How can we possibly expect anyone to find real nurture, comfort, and consolation from a prayer life that taxes the mind beyond its limits and adds one more exhausting activity to the many already scheduled ones?

During the last decade, many have discovered the limits of the intellect. More and more people have realized that what they need is much more than interesting sermons and interesting prayers. They wonder how they might really experience God. The charismatic movement is an obvious response to this new search for prayer. The popularity of Zen and the experimentation with encounter techniques in the churches are also indicative of a new desire to experience God. Suddenly we find ourselves surrounded by people saying, 'Teach us to pray.' And suddenly we become aware that we are being asked to show the way through a region that we do not know ourselves. The crisis of our prayer life is that our mind may be filled with ideas of God while our heart remains far from him. Real prayer comes from the heart. It is about this prayer of the heart that the Desert Fathers teach us.

The Prayer of the Heart

Hesychastic prayer, which leads to that rest where the soul can dwell with God, is prayer of the heart. For us who are so mind-oriented it is of special importance to learn to pray with and from the heart. The Desert Fathers can show us the way. Although they do not offer any theory about prayer, their concrete stories and counsels offer the stones with which the later Orthodox spiritual writers have built a very impressive spirituality. The spiritual writers of Mount Sinai, Mount Athos, and the *startsi* of nineteenth-century Russia are all anchored in the tradition of the desert. We find the best formulation of the prayer of the heart in the words of the Russian mystic Theophan the Recluse: 'To pray is to descend with the mind into the heart, and there to stand before the face of the Lord, ever-present, all-seeing, within you.'[2] All through the centuries, this view of prayer has been central in hesychasm. Prayer is standing in the presence of God with the mind in the heart; that is, at that point of our being where there are no divisions or distinctions and where we are totally one. There God's Spirit dwells and there the great encounter takes place. There heart speaks to heart, because there we stand before the face of the Lord, all-seeing, within us.

We have to realize that here the word heart is used in its full biblical meaning. In our milieu the word heart has become a soft word. It refers to the seat of the sentimental life. Expressions such as 'heartbroken' and 'heartfelt' show that we often think of the heart as the warm place where the emotions are located in contrast to the cool intellect where our thoughts find their home. But the word heart in the Jewish-Christian tradition refers to the source of all physical, emotional, intellectual, volitional, and moral energies.

From the heart arise unknowable impulses as well as conscious feelings, moods, and wishes. The heart, too, has its reasons and is the center of perception and understanding. Finally, the heart is the seat of the will: it makes plans and comes to good decisions. Thus the heart is the central and unifying organ of our personal life. Our heart determines our personality, and is therefore not only the place where God dwells but also the place to which Satan directs his fiercest attacks. It is this heart that is the place of prayer. The prayer of the heart is a prayer that directs itself to God from the center of the person and thus affects the whole of our humanness.

One of the Desert Fathers, Macarius the Great, says, 'The chief task of the athlete [that is, the monk] is to enter into his heart.'[3] This does not mean that the monk should try to fill his prayer with feeling, but that he should strive to let his prayer remodel the whole of his person. The most profound insight of the Desert Fathers is that entering into the heart is entering into the kingdom of God. In other words, the way to God is through the heart. Isaac the Syrian writes: 'Try to enter the treasure chamber . . . that is within you and then you will discover the treasure chamber of heaven. For they are one and the same. If you succeed in entering one, you will see both. The ladder to this Kingdom is hidden inside you, in your soul. If you wish your soul clean of sin you will see there the rungs of the ladder which you may climb.'[4] And John Carpathios says: 'It takes great effort and struggle in prayer to reach that state of mind which is free from all disturbance; it is a heaven within the heart [literally "endocardial"], the place, as the Apostle assures us, "where Christ dwells in us" (2 Cor. 13:5).'[5]

The Desert Fathers in their sayings point us toward a very holistic view of prayer. They pull us away from our intellectualizing practices, in which God becomes one of the many problems we have to address. They show us that real prayer penetrates to the marrow of our soul and leaves nothing untouched. The prayer of the heart is a prayer that does not allow us to limit our relationship with God to interesting words or pious emotions. By its very nature such prayer transforms our whole being into Christ precisely because it opens the eyes of our soul to the truth of ourselves as well as to the truth of God. In our heart we come to see ourselves as sinners embraced by the mercy of God. It is this vision that makes us cry out, 'Lord Jesus Christ, Son of the living God, have mercy on me, a sinner.' The prayer of the heart challenges us to hide absolutely nothing from God and to surrender ourselves unconditionally to his mercy.

Thus the prayer of the heart is the prayer of truth. It unmasks the many illusions about ourselves and about God and leads us into the true relationship of the sinner to the merciful God. This truth is what gives us the 'rest' of the hesychast. To the degree that this truth anchors itself in our heart, we will be less distracted by worldly thoughts and more single-mindedly directed toward the Lord of both our heart and the universe. Thus the words of Jesus, 'Happy the pure in heart: they shall see God' (Matthew 5:8), will become real in our prayer. Temptations and struggles will remain to the end of our lives, but with a pure heart we will be restful even in the midst of a restless existence.

This raises the question of how to practice the prayer of the heart in a very restless ministry. It is to this question of discipline that we must now turn our attention.

Prayer and Ministry

How can we, who are not monks and do not live in the desert, practice the prayer of the heart? How does the prayer of the heart affect our daily ministry?

The answer to these questions lies in the formulation of a definite discipline, a rule of prayer. There are three characteristics of the prayer of the heart that can help us to formulate this discipline:

- The prayer of the heart is nurtured by short, simple prayers.
- The prayer of the heart is unceasing.
- The prayer of the heart is all-inclusive.

Nurtured by Short Prayers

In the context of our verbose culture it is significant to hear the Desert Fathers discouraging us from using too many words: 'Abba Macarius was asked "How should one pray?" The old man said, "There is no need at all to make long discourses; it is enough to stretch out one's hand and say, 'Lord, as you will, and as you know, have mercy.' And if the conflict grows fiercer say: 'Lord, help.' He knows very well what we need and he shows us his mercy." '[6]

John Climacus is even more explicit: 'When you pray do not try to express yourself in fancy words, for often it is the simple, repetitious phrases of a little child that our Father in heaven finds most irresistible. Do not strive for verbosity lest your mind be distracted from devotion by a search for words. One phrase on the lips of the tax collector was enough to win God's mercy; one humble request made with faith was enough to save the good thief. Wordiness in prayer often subjects the mind to fantasy and dissipation; single words of their very nature tend to concentrate the mind. When you find satisfaction or compunction in a certain word of your prayer, stop at that point.'[7]

This is a very helpful suggestion for us, people who depend so much on verbal ability. The quiet repetition of a single word can help us to descend with the mind into the heart. This repetition has nothing to do with magic. It is not meant to throw a spell on God or to force him into hearing us. On the contrary, a word or sentence repeated frequently can help us to concentrate, to move to the center, to create an inner stillness and thus to listen to the voice of God. When we simply try to sit silently and wait for God to speak to us, we find ourselves bombarded with endless conflicting thoughts and ideas. But when we use a very simple sentence such as 'O God, come to my assistance,' or 'Jesus, master, have mercy on me,' or a word such as 'Lord' or 'Jesus,' it is easier to let the many distractions pass by without being misled by them. Such a simple, easily repeated prayer can slowly empty out our crowded interior life and create the quiet space where we can dwell with God. It can be like a ladder along which we can descend into the heart and ascend to God. Our choice of words depends on our needs and the circumstances of the moment, but it is best to use words from Scripture.

This way of simple prayer, when we are faithful to it and practice it at regular times, slowly leads us to an experience of rest and opens us to God's active presence. Moreover, we can take this prayer with us into a very busy day. When, for instance, we have spent twenty minutes in the early morning sitting in the presence of God with the words 'The Lord is my Shepherd' they may slowly build a little nest for themselves in our heart and stay there for the rest of our busy day. Even while we are talking, studying, gardening, or building, the prayer can continue in our heart and keep us aware of God's ever-present guidance. The discipline is not directed toward coming to a deeper insight into what it means that God is called our Shepherd, but toward coming to the inner experience of God's shepherding action in whatever we think, say, or do.

Unceasing

The second characteristic of the prayer of the heart is that it is unceasing. The question of how to follow

Paul's command to 'pray without ceasing' has had a central place in hesychasm from the time of the Desert Fathers to nineteenth-century Russia. There are many examples of this concern from both ends of the hesychastic tradition.

During the period of the Desert Fathers, there was a pietistic sect called the Messalians. These were people who had an overly spiritualized approach to prayer and considered manual work condemnable for a monk. Some of the monks of this sect went to see Abba Lucius. 'The old man asked them, "What is your manual work?" They said, "We do not touch manual work but as the Apostle says, we pray without ceasing." The old man asked them if they did not eat and they replied they did. So he said to them, "When you are eating who prays for you then?" Again he asked them if they did not sleep and they replied they did. And he said to them, "When you are asleep, who prays for you then?" They could not find any answer to give him. He said to them, "Forgive me, but you do not act as you speak. I will show you how, while doing my manual work, I pray without interruption. I sit down with God, soaking my reeds and plaiting my ropes, and I say, 'God, have mercy on me; according to your great goodness and according to the multitude of your mercies, save me from my sins.' " So he asked them if this were not prayer and they replied it was. Then he said to them, "So when I have spent the whole day working and praying, making thirteen pieces of money more or less, I put two pieces of money outside the door and I pay for my food with the rest of the money. He who takes the two pieces of money prays for me when I am eating and when I am sleeping; so, by the grace of God, I fulfill the precept to pray without ceasing." '[8]

This story offers a very practical answer to the question 'How can I pray without ceasing while I am busy with many other things?' The answer involves the neighbor. Through my charity my neighbor becomes a partner in my prayer and makes it into unceasing prayer.

In the nineteenth century, when the problems with the Messalians did not exist, a more mystical response was given. We find it in the famous story about a Russian peasant called *The Way of the Pilgrim*. It begins as follows: 'By the grace of God I am a Christian man, but by my actions a great sinner . . . On the twenty-fourth Sunday after Pentecost I went to church to say my prayers there during the Liturgy. The first Epistle of St. Paul to the Thessalonians was being read, and among other words I heard these – "*Pray without ceasing*" [1 Thessalonians 5:17]. It was this text, more than any other, which forced itself upon my mind, and I began to think how it was possible to pray without ceasing, since a man has to concern himself with other things also in order to make a living.'[9] The peasant went from church to church to listen to sermons but did not find the answer he desired. Finally he met a holy *staretz* who said to him: '"Ceaseless interior prayer is a continual yearning of the human spirit towards God. To succeed in this consoling exercise we must pray more often to God to teach us to pray without ceasing. Pray more, and pray more fervently. It is prayer itself which will reveal to you how it can be achieved unceasingly; but it will take some time."'[10] Then the holy *staretz* taught the peasant the Jesus Prayer: 'Lord Jesus Christ, have mercy on me.' While traveling as a pilgrim through Russia, the peasant repeats this prayer thousands of times with his lips. He even considers the Jesus Prayer to be his true companion. And then one day he has the feeling that the prayer by its own action passes from his lips to his heart. He says: '. . . it seemed as though my heart in its ordinary beating began to say the words of the Prayer within at each beat . . . I gave up saying the Prayer with my lips. I simply listened carefully to what my heart was saying.'[11]

Here we learn of another way of arriving at unceasing prayer. The prayer continues to pray within me even when I am talking with others or concentrating on manual work. The prayer has become the active presence of God's Spirit guiding me through life.

Thus we see how, through charity and the activity of the Prayer of Jesus in our heart, our whole day can become a continual prayer. I am not suggesting that we should imitate the monk Lucius or the Russian pilgrim, but I do suggest that we, too, in our busy ministry should be concerned to pray without ceasing, so that whatever we eat, whatever we drink, whatever we do at all, we do for the glory of God. (See 1 Cor. 10:31.) To love and work for the glory of God cannot remain an idea about which we think once in a while. It must become an interior, unceasing doxology.

All-inclusive

A final characteristic of the prayer of the heart is that it includes all our concerns. When we enter with our mind into our heart and there stand in the presence of God, then all our mental preoccupations become prayer. The power of the prayer of the heart is precisely that through it all that is on our mind becomes prayer.

When we say to people, 'I will pray for you,' we make a very important commitment. The sad thing is that this remark often remains nothing but a well-meant expression of concern. But when we learn to descend with our mind into our heart, then all those who have become part of our lives are led into the healing presence of God and touched by him in the center of our being. We are speaking here about a mystery for which words are inadequate. It is the mystery that the heart, which is the center of our being, is transformed by God into his own heart, a heart large enough to embrace the entire universe. Through prayer we can carry in our heart all human pain and sorrow, all conflicts and agonies, all torture and war, all hunger, loneliness, and misery, not because of some great psychological or emotional capacity, but because God's heart has become one with ours.

Here we catch sight of the meaning of Jesus' words, 'Shoulder my yoke and learn from me, for I am gentle and humble in heart, and you will find rest for your souls. Yes, my yoke is easy and my burden light' (Matthew 11:29–30). Jesus invites us to accept his burden, which is the burden of the whole world, a burden that includes human suffering in all times and places. But this divine burden is light, and we can carry it when our heart has been transformed into the gentle and humble heart of our Lord.

Here we can see the intimate relationship between prayer and ministry. The discipline of leading all our people with their struggles into the gentle and humble heart of God is the discipline of prayer as well as the discipline of ministry. As long as ministry only means that we worry a lot about people and their problems; as long as it means an endless number of activities which we can hardly coordinate, we are still very much dependent on our own narrow and anxious heart. But when our worries are led to the heart of God and there become prayer, then ministry and prayer become two manifestations of the same all-embracing love of God.

We have seen how the prayer of the heart is nurtured by short prayers, is unceasing and all-inclusive. These three characteristics show how the prayer of the heart is the breath of the spiritual life and of all ministry. Indeed, this prayer is not simply an important activity, but the very center of the new life which we want to represent and to which we want to introduce our people. It is clear from the characteristics of the prayer of the heart that it requires a personal discipline. To live a prayerful life we cannot do without specific prayers. We need to say them in such a way that we can listen better to the Spirit praying in us. We need to continue to include in our prayer all the people with and for whom we live and work. This discipline will help us to move from a distracting, fragmentary, and often frustrating ministry toward an integrating, holistic, and very gratifying ministry. It will not make ministry easy, but simple; it will not make it sweet and pious, but spiritual; it will not make it painless and without struggles, but restful in the true hesychastic sense.

Conclusion

In our mind-oriented world, we will need a serious discipline to come to a prayer of the heart in which we can listen to the guidance of Him who prays in us. The great emphasis on prayer in ministry is not meant as an incentive to be less involved with people or to leave untouched our society with its many struggles. Prayer as understood by the hesychasts helps us to discern which of our ministerial activities are indeed for the glory of God and which are primarily for the glory of our unconverted ego. The prayer of the heart offers us a new sensitivity that enables us to separate the chaff from the wheat in our ministry and thus to become much less ambiguous witnesses of Jesus Christ.

The prayer of the heart is indeed the way to the purity of heart that gives us eyes to see the reality of our existence. This purity of heart allows us to see more clearly, not only our own needy, distorted, and anxious self but also the caring face of our compassionate God. When that vision remains clear and sharp, it will be possible to move into the midst of a tumultuous world with a heart at rest. It is this restful heart that will attract those who are groping to find their way through life. When we have found our rest in God we can do nothing other than minister. God's rest will be visible wherever we go and whoever we meet. And before we speak any words, the Spirit of God, praying in us, will make his presence known and gather people into a new body, the body of Christ himself.

Epilogue

The question with which I started this exploration of desert spirituality and contemporary ministry was: 'How can we minister in an apocalyptic situation?' In a period of history dominated by the growing fear of a war that cannot be won and an increasing sense of impotence, the question of ministry is very urgent.

As a response to this question I have presented the words, 'Flee from the world, be silent and pray always,' words spoken to the Roman aristocrat Arsenius who asked God how to be saved. Solitude, silence, and unceasing prayer form the core concepts of the spirituality of the desert. I consider them to be of great value for us who are ministers as we approach the end of the second millennium of Christianity.

Solitude shows us the way to let our behavior be shaped not by the compulsions of the world but by our new mind, the mind of Christ. Silence prevents us from being suffocated by our wordy world and teaches us to speak the Word of God. Finally, unceasing prayer gives solitude and silence their real meaning. In unceasing prayer, we descend with the mind into the heart. Thus we enter through our heart into the heart of God, who embraces all of history with his eternally creative and recreative love.

But does not this spirituality of the desert close our eyes to the cruel realities of our time? No. On the contrary, solitude, silence, and prayer allow us to save ourselves and others from the shipwreck of our self-destructive society. The temptation is to go mad with those who are mad and to go around yelling and screaming, telling everyone where to go, what to do, and how to behave. The temptation is to become so involved in the agonies and ecstasies of the last days that we will drown together with those we are trying to save.

Jesus himself has warned us:

> 'Take care that no one deceives you; because many will come using my name and saying, "I am the Christ," and they will deceive many. You will hear of wars and rumors of wars; do not be alarmed, for this is something that must happen, but the end will not be yet. For nation will fight against nation, and kingdom against kingdom. There will be famines and earthquakes here and there . . . many will fall away; men will betray one another and hate one another. Many false prophets will arise; they will deceive many, and with the increase of lawlessness, love in most men will

> grow cold; but those who stand firm to the end will be saved. This Good News of the kingdom will be proclaimed to the whole world as a witness to all the nations. And then the end will come' (Matthew 24:4–14).

These words of Jesus have a striking relevance. It is our great task to stand firm to the end, to proclaim the Good News to the whole world, and to hold on to him who rose victorious from the grave. The raging torrents of our tumultuous times have made it very hard not to lose sight of the light and not to let ourselves drift away into the darkness. The powers and principalities not only reveal their presence in the unsettling political and economic situation of our day but also they show their disruptive presence in the most intimate places of our lives. Our faithfulness in relationships is severely tested, and our inner sense of belonging is questioned again and again. Our anger and greed show their strength with added vehemence, and our desire to indulge ourselves in the despairing hedonism of the moment proves to be stronger than ever.

Yes, the dangers are very real. It is not impossible that we might become false prophets shouting, 'Look, here is the Christ' or 'He is there' (Matthew 24:23). It is not impossible that we might deceive people with our self-made assurances, and that not only others' love but also our own might grow cold. Our compulsive, wordy, and mind-oriented world has a firm grip on us, and we need a very strong and persistent discipline not to be squeezed to death by it.

By their solitude, silence, and unceasing prayer the Desert Fathers show us the way. These disciplines will teach us to stand firm, to speak words of salvation, and to approach the new millennium with hope, courage, and confidence.

When we have been remodeled into living witnesses of Christ through solitude, silence, and prayer, we will no longer have to worry about whether we are saying the right thing or making the right gesture, because then Christ will make his presence known even when we are not aware of it.

Let me conclude with one more desert story.

'Three Fathers used to go and visit blessed Anthony every year and two of them used to discuss their thoughts and the salvation of their souls with him, but the third always remained silent and did not ask him anything. After a long time, Abba Anthony said to him: "You often come here to see me, but you never ask me anything," and the other replied, "It is enough to see you, Father." '[1]

This story is a fit ending to this book. By the time people feel that just seeing us is ministry, words such as these will no longer be necessary.

Notes

Prologue

1. Benedicta Ward, trans., *The Sayings of the Desert Fathers* (London & Oxford: Mowbrays, 1975), p. 8.

Solitude

1. Thomas Merton, *The Wisdom of the Desert* (New York: New Directions Publishing Corp., 1960), p. 3.
2. Benedicta Ward, trans., *The Sayings of the Desert Fathers* (London & Oxford: Mowbrays, 1975), p. 61.
3. Ibid., p. 2.
4. Ibid., pp. 2–5
5. Ibid., pp. 120–21.
6. Ibid.
7. Ibid., p. 117.
8. Ibid., p. 23.
9. Ibid., pp. 24–25.
10. Merton, *Wisdom of the Desert*, p. 23.
11. Ward, *Sayings of the Desert Fathers*, p. 6.

Silence

1. James O. Hannay, *The Wisdom of the Desert* (London: Methuen, 1904), p. 206.
2. Benedicta Ward, trans., *The Sayings of the Desert Fathers* (London & Oxford: Mowbrays, 1975), p. 69.
3. Thomas Merton, *The Way of Chuang Tzu* (New York: New Directions, 1965), p. 154.

4. Ward, *The Sayings of the Desert Fathers*, p. 198.
5. Hannay, *Wisdom of the Desert*, p. 205.
6. Diadochus of Photiki, 'On Spiritual Knowledge and Discrimination: One Hundred Texts,' in *The Philokalia*, vol. 1, compiled by St. Nikodimos of the Holy Mountain and St. Makarios of Corinth, trans., eds., G.E.H. Palmer, Phillip Sherrard, Kallistos Ware (London & Boston: Faber & Faber, 1979), p. 276.
7. Hannay, *Wisdom of the Desert*, pp. 205–206.
8. Vincent van Gogh, *The Complete Letters of Vincent van Gogh* (Greenwich, Connecticut: New York Graphic Society, 1959), vol. 1, p. 197.
9. Ward, *Sayings of the Desert Fathers*, p. 143.
10. Jean Bremond, *Les Pères Du Désert*, vol. 2 (Paris: Libraire Victor Lecoffre, 1927), p. 371.

Prayer

1. Benedicta Ward, trans., *The Sayings of the Desert Fathers* (London & Oxford: Mowbrays, 1975), p. 71.
2. Timothy Ware, ed. *The Art of Prayer: An Orthodox Anthology* (London: Faber & Faber, 1966), p. 110.
3. Macarius the Great, cited in Irenée Hausherr, *The Name of Jesus*, trans. Charles Cummings (Kalamazoo, MI: Cistercian Publications Inc., 1978), p. 314.
4. Ibid.
5. John Carpathios, cited in Hausherr, *The Name of Jesus*, p. 314.
6. Ward, *Sayings of the Desert Fathers*, p. 111.
7. John Climacus, cited in Hausherr, *The Name of Jesus*, p. 286.
8. Ward, *Sayings of the Desert Fathers*, p. 102.
9. R. M. French, trans., *The Way of the Pilgrim* (New York: The Seabury Press, 1965), p. 1.
10. Ibid., pp. 2–3.
11. Ibid., pp. 19–20.

Epilogue

1. Benedicta Ward, trans., *The Sayings of the Desert Fathers* (London & Oxford: Mowbrays, 1975), p. 6.